SERMONS ON THE HEALING MIRACLES OF JESUS

Sermons on the Healing Miracles of Jesus

PATRICK G. JONES

CAUTLEY HOUSE BOOKS

Hythe

First published 2003

Published by Cautley House Books
Cautley House Christian Centre, 95 Seabrook Road
Hythe, Kent, CT21 5QY.

ISBN 0 9544130 0 8

Book design and production for the publisher by
Bookprint Creative Services, P.O. Box 827, BN21 3YJ, England.
Printed in Great Britain.

Contents

Foreword

Cautley House has an important place in the ministry of health and healing, and in the hearts of a growing number of people who have benefited from its ministry. At the heart of this work has been the faithful preaching of the Word of hope alongside the ministry of prayer, and in this book we have some fine examples of that Christ-centred preaching.

Patrick Jones writes as he lives – with grace, generosity and compassion, wholly caught up with the abundant, inexhaustible love of God. Drawing on the riches of Jesus' own ministry among people in need, Patrick skilfully entwines the biblical narratives with the narratives of our own lives, and therefore always offers us encouragement and grounds for hope.

In these sermons there is challenge, insight, wisdom and above all, love – love of God and love of his people. No-one could read these short chapters without being drawn more closely into the orbit of a God who desires our well-being more than we can ever imagine, and who gives himself constantly to the task of healing his wounded world.

+ John Jarrow

Introduction

One of the greatest privileges afforded to a priest, is that of preaching the Good News of Jesus Christ. For the past thirty years I have enjoyed this privilege, and although many of my sermons and addresses have sadly fallen short of the mark, I rejoice that just occasionally there has been a sense that the Lord has used them.

It's humbling to have been asked for copies of my sermons preached over the years at Cautley House. However, to relieve our already overworked photocopier, it was suggested that a series of books of sermons be published, in the hope that others would find them helpful or thought-provoking.

Like most preachers, over the years I have gathered quotes, anecdotes and other material to help enliven my sermons and talks. I have to confess that, probably unlike most, I hardly ever remember where I discovered them or who wrote them, and I therefore apologise if I have used, quoted or mis-quoted without due acknowledgement.

May all glory be to Jesus Christ, the Living Word!

1

The Healing of Simon's Mother-in-law

Healed servants serving the healer

Mark 1:29–34

As soon as they left the synagogue, they entered the house of Simon and Andrew, with James and John. Now Simon's mother-in-law was in bed with a fever, and they told him about her at once. He came and took her by the hand and lifted her up. Then the fever left her, and she began to serve them.

That evening, at sundown, they brought to him all who were sick or possessed with demons. And the whole city was gathered around the door. And he cured many who were sick with various diseases, and cast out many demons; and he would not permit the demons to speak, because they knew him.

In this passage, we see that Jesus healed Simon's mother-in-law of a fever.

Now this might not seem like one of Jesus' more spectacular healings. After all, it can hardly be as important as healing someone of leprosy, or giving sight to a blind man, or even raising Lazarus from the dead. And yet the Gospel writer, Mark, thought it important enough to want to include it in his biography of Jesus.

On first glance, it could appear that the purpose of healing this woman of flu, might have been so that the men would have someone to prepare and serve them dinner! But that's hardly fair, is it? After all, Jesus was a champion of women's rights, and he always treated women with dignity and respect!

It's interesting to note, this incident took place on a Sabbath day. Earlier that morning, in the synagogue, Jesus had healed a badly troubled man and in so doing had emphasised his right to heal on the Sabbath. Now, for a second time, he's going to heal on the Sabbath. Jesus had made it clear that he considered that the Sabbath was made for human beings, and not human beings for the Sabbath. So let's picture the scene:

Jesus had been invited over to the house of Simon and Andrew, with James and John. They had just come from a worship service in the synagogue. Many scholars speculate that the house was right next door to the Synagogue, for as the text says, 'As soon as they left the Synagogue, they entered the house of Simon and Andrew.' This is the house where Simon Peter lived while he was in Capernaum. It was an open house for the disciples and Jesus, through the gracious hospitality of Peter's mother-in-law. I think it's reasonable to assume they were looking forward to putting their feet up and to a nice meal, that would be cooked for them with loving devotion – but this isn't why Jesus healed Peter's mother-in-law! Jesus healed this woman because he was concerned that she was suffering. It's clear that the disciples who were with Jesus were also concerned about her suffering because it says, 'they told him about her at once.' So let's be clear about this, Sabbath or no Sabbath, meal or no meal, Jesus' impulse to heal people was not for personal gain or glory, not for a meal, but out of his sheer love and compassion for people. That's what this miracle is about.

In a way, this miracle, like all other miracles, pre-empts Christ's death upon the cross – which was the act of love and compassion *par excellence*. For by his death at Calvary now anyone, at anytime, can bring their burdens to him. And it's as we remember his encouraging words: 'Come to me all that are weighed down with heavy burdens and I will give you rest,' that we take him at his word, and do just that. Whether it is to ask Jesus to heal us or others we care about, we have this longing for rest. Whether it is on our Sabbath or in the middle of the week, we feel compelled by our faith in his love, to ask for his healing touch.

It's good to remember that Jesus carried his divine power from the Synagogue to Peter's house where he healed Peter's mother-in-law. Like Jesus, we make our way from our place of worship to our own homes, but it's a fair question to ask, 'How far does the inspiration of a service get carried with us? How soon is it before we lay aside any inspiration from a service and become totally absorbed into the many claims of everyday life?'

You see, the inspiration and influence from an act of worship is meant to be applied in our daily interests and efforts, and the power of God, proclaimed in an act of worship should be a power we never lose. It is something always to be held in our hearts as a source of inspiration and a guide for daily living. What a shame it is, that many people leave behind at the church or chapel door, the influence of an act of worship. Because it's such a blessing when we allow Christ to move beyond the worship experience into our hearts, our homes and our communities.

Peter's mother-in-law was healed by Jesus in her home, and then she began to serve him and his disciples immediately afterwards. So here she was, so grateful for what he had done, and in response she simply wanted to serve the great healer himself – not out of some sense of drudgery and duty, but out of an overwhelming sense of gratitude and love. It prompts us to ask what our motivation is for serving Jesus. Is it duty? Or is it out of gratitude and love?

There are one or two things to notice about this miracle.

Firstly, if we are tempted to call this one of the 'lesser miracles' of Jesus, we would do well to remember that although it may not be as dramatic as some of the others, this is often how we approach Jesus with a request to intervene in our daily lives. Sometimes a prayer to Jesus might simply be a prayer that we make it through another day, or perhaps a prayer that we might have an increased peace, an inner serenity, or simply help in becoming a nicer person who doesn't blow-up at others so easily.

You see there's no such thing as lesser or greater miracles. Of course, some may be more dramatic like the raising of Lazarus from the dead, or even Jesus' own resurrection, but the main point is that whenever Jesus heals, he heals out of love and compassion – and he doesn't have a sliding scale of importance. How often I hear people say that they wouldn't ask God to bring healing to a particular situation, because it's not as serious as some of the things others have to cope with. But Jesus heals out of love and compassion.

Surely our response, should always be wanting to serve him out of a profound sense of love and gratitude.

Jesus' love is so powerful, and his healing so unique, that if we invite his healing presence into our own lives, and we devote ourselves to following him, we become true disciples. This is what makes being a Christian so exciting. We discover the truth that it's in giving that we receive.

Sadly, we all know how easy it is to forget Jesus. We can become so involved in each of our personal interests and pursuits, that Jesus can be squeezed out so that we don't even sense his absence. This is what happened to Samson in the Old Testament; he'd been so blessed by God and yet by his own neglect somehow he lost contact with God. It happened so gradually and silently that we are told, 'he did not know that the Lord had departed from him' (Judges 16:20)

So let's welcome Jesus. Let's worship him and be reassured that he can and will meet all our needs, no matter how important or trivial we may think they are.

Let's allow ourselves to be healed by Jesus the healer, and then turn around and live a humble life of gratitude serving him. There can be no greater honour than this, for we become all that God meant us to be.

Along with Peter's mother-in-law, we are healed servants of God, called into discipleship, which is a service of healing and of proclaiming God's good news for everyone.

2

Jesus Heals at the Pool of Bethesda

Why are some not healed?

John 5:1–9

After this there was a festival of the Jews, and Jesus went up to Jerusalem.

Now in Jerusalem by the Sheep Gate there is a pool, called in Hebrew Beth-zatha, which has five porticoes. In these lay many invalids – blind, lame, and paralysed. One man was there who had been ill for thirty-eight years. When Jesus saw him lying there and knew that he had been there a long time, he said to him, 'Do you want to be made well?' The sick man answered him, 'Sir, I have no one to put me into the pool when the water is stirred up; and while I am making my way, someone else steps down ahead of me.' Jesus said to him, 'Stand up, take your mat and walk.' At once the man was made well, and he took up his mat and began to walk.

Jeremiah 8:22

Is there no balm in Gilead? Is there no physician there? Why then has the health of my poor people not been restored?

At the pool of Bethesda by the Sheep Gate in Jerusalem, hundreds were sick and dying. Jesus healed just one of them. What about the rest of those people? As far as we can tell from John's story, they were left in their misery. I think if we are ever going to deal honestly with the topic of healing, we have to deal with this troubling subject; why are some not healed?

We have certainly prayed for people in the Cautley House chapel, and they have been healed. And yet there have been many others for whom we have prayed – and they have died! We all have our own stories, and we often share our frustration and concern about those who are on our current prayer list, who don't seem to be getting any better. I guess many of us echo the words of Jeremiah, when he cried, 'Is there no balm in Gilead? Is there no physician there? Why then has the health of my poor people not been restored?'

In Jeremiah's day, the town of Gilead was a symbol of hope. It was a centre for medical treatment, and was specially known for its healing ointments. If there's no healing balm in Gilead, then there's no hope to found anywhere. This is the cry of one who has tried everything and come up with nothing. I guess some of us can relate to Jeremiah's cry.

So what's going on when healing doesn't appear to be happening? I think we begin with an identity issue. God is the healer, not us! So if healing isn't happening in the way we think it should, we may need to take another look at our passports, and remind ourselves of who we are. Let's be honest, most of us, when we pray for healing, want to decide the outcome. We want to decide who is healed, and when and how. And if the healing doesn't happen in the way we want it to, or in our time-scale, then we have the tendency to think that there was something wrong with how we prayed, or God doesn't really care as deeply as we thought he did. Our prayers have failed!

Now, we have a control issue here, that we need to recognise. Christian healing isn't magic. We can't wave a magic wand to suspend the operation of the universe in order that our own purposes might be served. We are not God! We are mere mortals. God alone is the healer. So that's the identity issue.

Then we have the failure issue. We human beings tend to look at life in terms of success and failure. If our prayers aren't answered in the way we want, then it seems as if our prayers have failed. But there's no such thing as failure in prayers for healing. God is always at work, and whenever we pray for someone, something always happens. It just may not be what we thought it would be. We put a very high priority on physical healing, but it may well be that there's something even more important that God has in mind. While we are thinking about, and looking for a physical healing, God may be working on a person's heart, healing an old wound, or transforming bitterness into love.

It may be that, through our prayers for healing, someone will come to know Jesus Christ for the first time in their life. Just think about it, physical healing, even at its very best, is still only temporary. Even the healthiest people amongst us will eventually die. But being healed spiritually will last beyond this life and into all eternity.

We have a tendency to think of death as the final tragedy. And of course, there are many times when death comes prematurely, and it seems so unfair to those who are left behind. But even in death there is healing. It's the journey that finally takes us home. God is always at work, but not always in ways we can see or understand. So when we pray for healing, it's good to approach God with humility, acknowledging that he is God, and we're not.

Now although we don't make healing happen, we're not entirely helpless in this process either. In our prayers for ourselves and for others, there are things we do that can either help or hinder the healing process. One of the things that hinders, is resistance. People may sometimes be resistant to healing – and that sounds strange, doesn't it?

There are two kinds of resistance: one is disbelief – a lack of openness to the ways of God. Healing requires faith. Not necessarily on the part of the one who is sick, but there must be faith involved somewhere in the process. I have to be honest with you; this faith business makes me nervous because how do we know if we have enough faith? I've heard people say that David Watson died because those praying for him didn't have enough faith. But that's simply not true!

Jesus said that faith, even the size of a mustard seed, is enough to move mountains. And you can stake your life on that! A mustard seed – that's about as big as a full stop at the end of a sentence! If a person has enough faith to come to God in prayer, to ask and to seek, then that's certainly as big as a mustard seed. And if we come to God with that mustard seed faith, then God is at work, though perhaps in ways we can't see or understand.

So even a tiny bit of faith can move mountains, but an atmosphere of disbelief is paralysing. The Gospels tell us that even Jesus, powerful as he was, couldn't do any miracles when he went home to Nazareth, because of their lack of faith. To them, Jesus was nothing special. He was just another local lad. They thought he was no more special than any of the other local lads. So they scoffed at him, and created an atmosphere of disbelief. They even called him 'Joseph's son', which to us sounds OK, but they did it in a mocking way to suggest that there was nothing remarkable or miraculous about how he came into the world. Healing was lacking in Nazareth, because they were resistant to it.

Besides disbelief, there's another kind of resistance that hinders the healing process. And this is an uncooperative attitude. Jesus asked the man by the pool of Bethesda, 'Do you want to be healed?' He didn't say, 'Do you believe I can do it?' but, 'Do you want it.'

You can't imagine anyone not wanting to be well, can you? But think back to when you were a child. Do you ever remember trying to make your mum or dad think you were sick, so you wouldn't have to go to school or do your chores. Or maybe you extended your cold or flu just a little, to get the attention and stay in bed. Did you ever 'phone in sick' so you wouldn't have to go to work? When you're sick, people have to take care of you. When you're well, you have to take care of yourself. In other words, well-ness carries responsibilities with it. This man by the pool hadn't been able to work in thirty-eight years. He hadn't been able to put out the dustbins, clean the garage, or help with the dishes. If he gets healed, he will have to take responsibility for his life.

It reminds me of the man who went to the doctor and explained that he wasn't able to do the things around the house that he used to do. After the doctor had given him a physical examination, the man said, 'Now doctor, I can take it. Tell me in plain English what's wrong with me?' 'OK, in plain English,' the doctor answered, 'You're just bone idle!'

'Well thank you for your honesty,' the man said, 'Now can you give me the medical term for this so I can explain it to my wife?'

If we want to be well, we need to be honest with ourselves and we need to co-operate with the healing process. God heals in many ways. Sometimes he works in dramatic and supernatural ways. Sometimes he works in some very natural and un-dramatic ways – for example, through rest and exercise, through doctors and counsellors, through surgery and medicine. It's our responsibility to co-operate with the healing process.

Sometimes it's clear that there are those who won't change their life-style, or won't take their medicine.

No matter how often they come up for the laying-on of hands or anointing, if God is calling them to a more wholesome lifestyle, and they resist it, then healing is hindered.

It also helps if we look for healing in the right place. The pool of Bethesda was thought to have magical powers, so people gathered there daily. Some went there every day for years, like the man that Jesus healed. The amazing thing is, while everyone else was focused on the magic pool, Jesus, the author of life, was walking among them, ready to reach out and touch and heal. As long as their eyes were on the pool, they wouldn't see Jesus.

So often we look for healing in the wrong place. Instead of looking for God to heal, we hope for a bit of magic. That's why alcoholics and drug addicts get hooked. That's why people who are depressed often over-eat chocolate and ice cream. It's not a hope for real healing, but for a little magic to make the pain go away. And magic, like the pool of Bethesda, is mostly an illusion. Real healing isn't the same as a quick fix. Genuine healing may well happen over a lifetime.

So to experience God's healing for ourselves and others, we need to re-focus our thoughts and energies. We need to turn away from illusions and quick fixes, and turn to the source of life – and that's the person of Jesus Christ. We need to trust God who loves us and works for our best, even when we can't see it.

3
Jesus Heals Ten Lepers
'Your faith has made you well'

Luke 17:11–19

On the way to Jerusalem Jesus was going through the region between Samaria and Galilee. As he entered a village, ten lepers approached him. Keeping their distance, they called out, saying, 'Jesus, Master, have mercy on us!' When he saw them, he said to them, 'Go and show yourselves to the priests.' And as they went, they were made clean. Then one of them, when he saw that he was healed, turned back, praising God with a loud voice. He prostrated himself at Jesus' feet and thanked him. And he was a Samaritan. Then Jesus asked, 'Were not ten made clean? But the other nine, where are they? Was none of them found to return and give praise to God except this foreigner?' Then he said to him, 'Get up and go on your way; your faith has made you well.'

'Go on your way, your faith has made you well.' We see the leper in the Gospel reading healed from his disease and Jesus

22

pronouncing this blessing on him, 'your faith has made you well.' Actually, the literal translation of those words is 'your faith has saved you.' And if we allow those words 'saved', and 'made well' to percolate for a while in our minds, I think we begin to arrive at an understanding of what people feel the Christian life is all about.

For example, there are some who would say, 'If my faith is real, then I'm saved, I'm well, I'm whole – things are OK, and I'm OK. But if I don't feel well, if I'm struggling, if I've failed in some way and don't feel very whole, then I have a spiritual crisis on my hands. How genuine can my faith really be? There goes that healed leper – his faith made him well. Why doesn't my faith work like that? Why aren't things OK with me? Maybe it's because I don't really have any faith!'

When a person becomes a Christian; when he or she is initiated in the Christian faith, what exactly are they being initiated into? What can they expect from it? It seems to me, there are two extremes that Christians fall into, as they look at their expectations. The truth lies somewhere in the middle.

The first extreme is the lack of any expectation at all. And I think this is a real position of many Christians. They don't expect that believing in Jesus Christ and belonging to his Church makes any fundamental difference to them. This doesn't mean that there are no benefits, otherwise why would anyone become a Christian? After all, there are needs that are met by belonging to the Christian Church – the need for acceptance and the need to belong to a community – but these needs tend to be psychological and aesthetic, rather than religious like wholeness and healing or salvation.

I guess that there are many who feel that whatever benefits a person may receive from being a Christian, it's an individual matter. But I'm uncomfortable with all of this. If being a Christian makes no real spiritual difference, why belong at all? And what's the point of the Gospel reading we've just heard?

What's the point of reading about people being changed by their encounter with Jesus if it can never happen to us?

I guess these questions lead us directly to what we mean by 'faith'? Why did Jesus say to the leper that it was his faith that made him well? Jesus didn't commend this poor chap for some powerful inner religious ability he had, or because he had some mystical knowledge of divine things. Jesus commended him for seeing in himself (Jesus), God was present and available to him. It was because he saw this, that he came to Jesus for help. Surely, that's what the Christian faith is all about? It's the seeing, it's the believing that in Jesus God is still making himself available to people. And it's on the basis of that recognition we simply come to Jesus. If Jesus is where God is, then to find God, we need to get close to Jesus. We need to follow him, learn to do what he does, listen to what he says – that's what it means to be a disciple, a student of the Master.

But what do those who come to Jesus and learn to be his disciples, look like? I think those who come close to him, who follow the Master, do begin to see some kind of change taking place in their lives. It's sometimes assumed by non-Christians, and even by some Christians, that being a Christian means you have it all together; that being a Christian means you've been made whole and complete, as if all the answers to all the needs are found in following Christ and through membership of his Church. But it can't be true. A Christian writer called Philip Yancey, wrote in one of his books, 'Alas, life with God often turns out to involve far more struggle and ambiguity than is sometimes advertised.' And we all know what that means, don't we? Because we know that none of us have got it 'all together'. No one I have ever met, including myself can be said to be completely whole and well. We all suffer brokenness to some degree. Being a Christian doesn't mean that we are immune from things like divorce, illness, bereavement, loneliness or anxiety.

What faith in Christ means, is that if a person lives in and with God, there will always be a difference. If God is available to us in Christ, in such a way as to be intimately involved with us, sharing his own life with us, everything must be different. Not that any Christ-follower ever reaches perfection in this life; not that any Christ-follower ever reaches a point when they never need to repent, but as a person learns to walk with Jesus, so they learn to trust him.

Jesus didn't promise that we would never know pain or anxiety, but he did promise that he would be in it with us. Sometimes he changes our difficult circumstances, as he did with the leper, and sometimes he changes us so that the difficult circumstances don't have the last word. By his blessèd presence in our lives, we are strengthened to live with whatever life throws at us, and are enabled to become more than conquerors through him who loves us.

So we come to encounter Jesus, trusting not in faith but in him, and in his good purposes for us.

4

Jesus Heals the Gerasene Demoniac
'What are you afraid of?'

Luke 8:26–37

Then they arrived at the country of the Gerasenes, which is opposite Galilee. As he stepped out on land, a man of the city who had demons met him. For a long time he had worn no clothes, and he did not live in a house but in the tombs. When he saw Jesus, he fell down before him and shouted at the top of his voice, 'What have you to do with me, Jesus, Son of the Most High God? I beg you, do not torment me' – for Jesus had commanded the unclean spirit to come out of the man. (For many times it had seized him; he was kept under guard and bound with chains and shackles, but he would break the bonds and be driven by the demon into the wilds.) Jesus then asked him, 'What is your name?' He said, 'Legion'; for many demons had entered him. They begged him not to order them to go back into the abyss.

Now there on the hillside a large herd of swine was feeding; and the demons begged Jesus to let them enter these. So he gave them permission. Then the demons came out of the man and entered the swine, and the herd rushed down the steep bank into the lake and was drowned. When the swineherds saw what had happened, they ran off and told it in the city and in the country. Then people came out to see what had happened, and when they came to Jesus, they found the man from whom the demons had gone sitting at the feet of Jesus, clothed and in his right mind. And they were afraid. Those who had seen it told them how the one who had been possessed by demons had been healed. Then all the people of the surrounding country of the Gerasenes asked Jesus to leave them; for they were seized with great fear.

In the story of the encounter Jesus had with a demon-possessed man, we are told that the residents of that area were afraid. But I wonder what they were afraid of? This is an important question, because there's a very distinct relationship between fear and faith. Throughout the Gospel narratives – in fact throughout the Bible, it seems to be a common experience that people have to pass through fear in order to experience the power of God. And that takes faith!

Consider Moses, that great hero of the Exodus; one day he comes across a burning bush in the desert. Although it's on fire it's not consumed and from the bush Moses hears the voice of God, and we're told he's afraid. And yet he had to overcome his fear in order to hear what God was saying, and that took faith. Hundreds of years later, there were shepherds out in the fields, keeping watch over the flocks by night. Suddenly an angel of the Lord appeared to them, and the glory of the Lord shone around them, and we are told they were 'sore afraid'. The shepherds had to overcome their fear to discover the miracle of the babe in the manger – and that took faith.

Whenever people had an encounter with God, it would seem they always had to pass through human fear. Mary was afraid when Gabriel announced that she was to be the mother of the Messiah. Joseph was afraid when he heard the news. Even at the resurrection as one by one the disciples encountered the empty tomb and the Risen Christ we are told they were afraid.

So it would seem there's a relationship between fear and faith. It's as if fear is the 'front door' to faith. It's as if you have to take fear by the handle and open that door to see what's on the other side, in order to experience the power of God.

Going back to the Gospel reading, we have to ask what the people of Gadera were afraid of. To begin with, it looks as if they were afraid of the appearance of the man possessed by demons – his demeanour. The man is identified by the name 'Legion', and Luke tells us that he's been given that name because he is possessed by a legion of demons – meaning a whole lot of demons! Luke is telling us that this man is really messed up!

Presumably this man was so possessed, that it provoked all sorts of bizarre behaviour. To try and keep this crazy man under control, they had to put him in chains and leg irons. But so strong was he, that he broke these restraints and ran around wildly. He was on the loose, living in the local cemetery. Luke says this tormented man was running around without a stitch of clothing on, shouting and howling. No wonder the people were afraid – who wouldn't be? And yet the text indicates that this bizarre behaviour wasn't what they were afraid of. So what were they afraid of?

There's another theory that says the people were afraid because when Jesus cast the demons out he let them go into a herd of pigs that stampeded over a cliff, presumably to their death. Although the Jewish followers of Jesus wouldn't have been bothered by this – because they considered pigs to be unclean, the Gentiles on the other hand – especially those who owned the pigs – now they would have been scared!

But notice how Luke describes the situation:

When the herdsmen saw what had happened, they fled and told it in the city and in the country. Then the people went out to see what had happened and they came to Jesus, and found the man from whom the demons had gone, sitting at the feet of Jesus, clothed, and in his right mind. And they were afraid!

Did you spot it? They found the man clothed and in his right mind, and they were afraid!

I think this passage captures a great truth. The truth, that sometimes it's easier for us to deal with people as being sick, or disabled, or even evil, than it is to deal with them being well, whole, redeemed!

I think this is why one of the most popular shows on TV today is *The Weakest Link*. Anne Robinson, who hosts the show, this hard and stern woman has become something of an icon to the millions who enjoy hearing her sarcastically telling the contestants off. She's highly skilled at insulting people, hurting them. And people love it! They wait for that moment of dismissal when she actually recites her now-famous words, 'You are the weakest link. Goodbye!' The contestant leaves in silence on what is called the 'walk of shame'.

Why are so many attracted to this sort of thing? Or to the *Big Brother* or *Survivor* type of programme, where people's flaws become the basis on which they are judged? There seems to be some strange sort of comfort that comes from seeing people in terms of their weaknesses and failings.

I believe that's why many who, when they tell their friends or relatives that they have become a Christian, find that they become objects of ridicule. People are often uncomfortable when they hear someone has found a new relationship with God. They seem to be more afraid of what it means to be well, than what it meant to be the way they were before. It's easier to embrace the brokenness they know, than the wholeness that is offered through the love and power of Jesus Christ.

That's why a man I know, who for so long had been in the grip of alcoholism, found it easier to see himself as a weak person, dominated by the power of alcohol, than as a good person, who with the help of God, could begin the process of recovery and wellness. He was less afraid of living with the bottle, than he was, living without it. He was afraid of becoming well.

Isn't this perhaps why many of us have such a difficult time doing the things we need to do, to be reconciled with someone? It's far easier to remain angry with someone than to forgive them. Somehow we can be more comfortable with the ulcers and psychic pain that comes from internalised bitterness and hurt, than we are with the possibility of a restored friendship. Sometimes it's scarier to be well, than to be sick!

On a global level, could it be that there are many who find it easier to see people as the enemy, rather than as potential friends; that they are afraid of making the world well?

In the middle of all this fear steps Jesus of Nazareth, the most amazing man who ever lived. He has a different vision of the world! He doesn't see humanity as being locked in sin, shame and sickness, but rather as potential recipients of the merciful and healing power of God. In the Gospel reading, Jesus is sitting there, between what Legion used to be, and what Legion has now become by the power of God – happy, whole and restored to his family and community. But the people are afraid – afraid because it means that they too can become healed; healed in their marriages, in their relationships, from their sicknesses, in their daily living as human beings.

Today, Jesus looks you and me straight in the eye and dares us to adopt a new vision for ourselves, our families, our neighbours and our world. Jesus invites us to see the world in terms of what it can become by the power of God!

Today, I want to encourage you to envision yourself as a perfect person – the kind of person God created you to be. A

perfect husband, a perfect wife, in the eyes of God. A perfect
parent in the eyes of God; a perfect friend, a perfect church
member in the eyes of God; a perfect neighbour in the eyes of
God. What would such a person look like in real terms? How
would they conduct themselves in their relationships? What
would they say, what would they do? To be completely honest
with you, it makes me feel very uncomfortable to think of
myself in those terms. I am afraid of becoming the person God
wants me to be. But so was Moses! So were the shepherds! So
was Mary, Joseph, the disciples, the demoniac named Legion –
they were all afraid too!

By facing their fear, they took the leap of faith, and took
hold of God's vision for their lives, and God led them to higher
places of living.

Whenever you or I step from fear to faith, God always inter-
venes – he won't let us down. Just think what he's calling us to!

5

Jesus Heals a Paralytic

The power of forgiveness

Mark 2:1–12

When Jesus returned to Capernaum after some days, it was reported that he was at home. So many gathered around that there was no longer room for them, not even in front of the door; and he was speaking the word to them. Then some people came, bringing to him a paralysed man, carried by four of them. And when they could not bring him to Jesus because of the crowd, they removed the roof above him; and after having dug through it, they let down the mat on which the paralytic lay. When Jesus saw their faith, he said to the paralytic, 'Son, your sins are forgiven.' Now some of the scribes were sitting there, questioning in their hearts, 'Why does this fellow speak in this way? It is blasphemy! Who can forgive sins but God alone?' At once Jesus perceived in his spirit that they were discussing these questions among themselves; and he said to them, 'Why do you raise such questions in your hearts? Which is easier, to say to the paralytic, "Your sins are forgiven," or to say, "Stand

*up and take your mat and walk?" But so that you may know
that the Son of Man has authority on earth to forgive sins' – he
said to the paralytic, 'I say to you, stand up, take your mat and
go to your home.' And he stood up, and immediately took the
mat and went out before all of them; so that they were all
amazed and glorified God, saying, 'We have never seen
anything like this!'*

The little seaside town of Capernaum was in uproar. That
young carpenter from Nazareth is back in town. He's been away
for some months, but now he's returned. Whilst he was away,
the talk of the town was about the incredible miracles he was
performing, and the new powerful ideas he had been teaching.
But now he's back, and apparently he's at Peter's house.

This is the event of the year in this sleepy backwater. There's
talk about him preaching and then healing a man who was out
of his mind, and of healing Peter's own mother-in-law. But
now he's at this house and everybody, but everybody, is there.
He's just finished his teaching when suddenly a man is being
lowered through a hole in the roof, and his stretcher comes to
rest right there at the feet of Jesus. People are whispering, one
to another, 'Hey, it's that guy who has been paralysed from
birth – you know, the one who lies on the porch of that little
fishing hut down at the water's edge.' Everyone is stunned – it's
not every day you see someone lowered through a roof. But
stranger is what happens next. At other times, Jesus simply
healed people – but this time, he doesn't. He just stands there
and says, 'My son, your sins are forgiven.' And the man stands
up straight!

We can't help but wonder; what in the world does the forgiving of sins have to do with someone standing up straight? To
find some understanding, we need to understand firstly, that
this story is not only about Jesus, but it's also about those who
hung out with him – that is, his disciples and the crowd.

In fact, to understand what's going on here, I'm tempted to ask you, 'Where are you in the story? Are you a disciple? Are you simply one of the crowds? Perhaps you are one of the healed man's helpers?' Whoever you are you'd be wrestling with, and maybe haunted by, the issue of forgiveness. Why is forgiveness so powerful that it can make a paralysed man walk again? And who is this man who can offer such power, and what does it have to do with us?

Imagine you are one of the crowd. It's been a dull week – maybe storms have prevented the fishing boats from leaving the little harbour. Perhaps it's been one of those weeks that you want to be over but in reality it's just dragged on. Then this so-called magician comes to town – it's the best entertainment ever, and it's free! You see the crowds getting angry, especially the scribes on their high horses. And now this upstart carpenter tells the man he's forgiven. Who is this man Jesus to forgive sins? He didn't even check to see if the man wanted forgiveness.

Then, I think, what do most people think about this business of forgiveness? If I'm sick, what do I care about God's forgiveness? I just want to get well! If I've lost my job, what difference does God's love make to me? I just want my job back! If I'm fat, ugly and don't like myself, what do I care about God's grace? I just want to be acceptable. If I'm unhappy about how life is treating me, what difference does God's concern about me make? I just want justice! In short, forgiveness seems to have nothing to with modern life. Consequently, when we hear that God is a forgiving God, many of us are unlikely to take it seriously and we look elsewhere for answers to our situation. And yet the story indicates that our very health and well-being depends somehow on forgiveness – that we need forgiveness if we are to stand tall.

When you think about it, the word 'righteousness' is on almost every page of the Bible. Righteousness simply means 'right relationship' – it means doing the right things to be in a right relationship; doing whatever is necessary to be 'right' in a relationship with God, with other people and with ourselves.

Take ourselves, for example. Most of us don't feel we are in a right relationship with ourselves. We need to feel, and to know, that we are of value – that we are not nobodies, but that we are somebodies. So many today, feel that there's something wrong about themselves; that they should be better than they are – more beautiful, more handsome, more intelligent, more talented. Many feel so inadequate – and there's an unspoken kind of shame about them. These kinds of feelings make people depressed, if not downright sick. So many of us just can't forgive ourselves for being ourselves. Wanting forgiveness simply means, 'I want to start again.' Forgiveness can enable us to start a new life, or take a new direction.

I guess we all know people who, because of their unforgiven past, are negative people. I certainly meet many who carry their bad memories and old grudges as if they are cherished possessions, They refuse to consider starting all over again with themselves, and as a result they become quite bitter. And the bitterness spreads around them wherever they go, poisoning a life that could be wonderful and beautiful. And instead of standing tall, they seem always to be knocked down by life.

Forgiveness is so important. It's a lifestyle, it's a state of being, it's a constant way of approaching life. It's not letting what you believe to be true to stand in the way of a greater truth, which is, that every single person, including yourself, is valuable and precious because they are loved by God.

Let me ask you a question. Can you let go of anything that happened yesterday, long enough to start all over again? When you started to read this chapter or this page, did you want to start a new relationship with God, and with anyone else? Today, can you leave behind anything of yesterday that was negative, or unwholesome? Can you leave behind any feelings of remorse or pessimism and move into a new beginning?

If you want to be a 'resurrection person'; if you want to start all over again, to know yourself to be forgiven, then repent and start again. The Lord, who is truly present beckons you to walk into a new life.

6

The Healing of Blind Bartimaeus

'What do you want from me?'

Mark 10:46–52

They came to Jericho. As Jesus and his disciples and a large crowd were leaving Jericho, Bartimaeus son of Timaeus, a blind beggar, was sitting by the roadside. When he heard that it was Jesus of Nazareth, he began to shout out and say, 'Jesus, Son of David, have mercy on me!' Many sternly ordered him to be quiet, but he cried out even more loudly, 'Son of David, have mercy on me.' Jesus stood still and said, 'Call him here.' And they called the blind man, saying to him, 'Take heart; get up, he is calling you.' So throwing off his cloak, he sprang up and came to Jesus. Then Jesus said to him, 'What do you want me to do for you?' The blind man said to him, 'My teacher, let me see again.' Jesus said to him, 'Go; your faith has made you well.' Immediately he regained his sight and followed him on the way.

Many years ago, when I became the vicar of my first parish, I remember having this very strange kind of experience. There was this young chap who lived in the parish – everyone knew him. He was a genuinely nice person, but just a bit on the quirky side of things. He had a habit, every time he saw me walking round the parish, he would spread his arms wide and yell at the top of his voice, 'There's Patrick Jones, he's the new vicar!'

It didn't take too long for this to get a bit tiresome, and it didn't take too long for me to start ducking into a shop when I saw him coming, or to head off in the opposite direction. Now I know he was a bit odd, and didn't mean any harm, but I used to find it so embarrassing because everyone used to stop and look whenever he shouted out. To be truthful, it began to get annoying. It irritated me, and I really wished he would stop it and leave me alone. One day it caught me on the raw, and I know it wasn't very Christian of me, but I snapped at him, 'Look, what do you want from me?'

I wonder if anything like that has happened to you? Someone behaving in such a way that it becomes a real nuisance – maybe one of your children, a friend or an associate? But someone keeps pestering you, especially in public, drawing unwanted attention to you. And you finally lose it to the point of saying, 'Look, what do you want from me?'

Now we don't know for sure, because the Gospel writer doesn't go into detail, but I have a feeling deep down, that we are in that kind of situation here in the Gospel reading with old Bartimaeus.

Jesus had come to Jericho and we are not told if anything special happened while he was there but now he's just about to leave and he's followed by a large crowd. Jesus is now at that point in his ministry where it was virtually impossible for him to go anywhere without crowds following, and so we get a sense of Jesus here as a public figure. He's very much in the public eye, and this makes the story all the more interesting.

He's heading out of town and Bartimaeus, son of Timaeus, is sitting there by the side of the road, and he's blind. As soon as he gets the buzz from the crowd that Jesus is passing by, he starts yelling at the top of his voice, 'Jesus, son of David, have mercy on me!'

You know, it's a little inappropriate to be sitting in the dirt by the side of the road screaming at the Messiah. Obviously the disciples think so too, because they reprimand him sternly and try to get him to be quiet. But old Bartimaeus has learned that the squeaky wheel may not always get the grease, but it does get noticed. And he screams even more loudly, 'Jesus, son of David! Have mercy on me!' Finally Jesus senses that he's not going to get out of this one. The text says, he 'stands still' and sends his disciples back down the road to get blind Bartimaeus. His friends say to him, 'Nice going, Bart, he's calling you.' So Bartimaeus throws off his cloak and stands up and faces Jesus. I wonder if Jesus gave a tired sigh as he says, 'What do you want from me?' Bartimaeus doesn't have to think about this one, he says, 'Master, let me see again.' Jesus says, 'Go. Your faith has made you well.' And immediately the man was healed and followed Jesus on the way.

I think this is a wonderful story because it offers us two really important things. Firstly, for me, this is a very human Jesus. This is Jesus who might be tired; a Jesus who may just be at the end of a long day. A Jesus who may not want to be the centre of attention at that moment, and yet is confronted with a situation where he has no choice but to act. It's a story that brings the grit of day to day life to the reality of the Incarnation, to the truth of God with us – and I like it! Sometimes I think it's hard to get our heads and our hearts around the image of a perfect Jesus. I guess we've all been told, 'No one was perfect, except Jesus, now go and be like him!'

But it's hard isn't it? Or I should say it's impossible to be like this perfect, no mistakes, God-like Jesus who we are supposed to imitate. But the Jesus in this story, a tired Jesus – now he's one I can deal with. A Jesus, who gets frustrated with his friends

and followers when they mess things up or just don't understand, and he rolls his eyes and says, 'How long must I endure
them?' A person like that I can relate to. A Jesus who simply
loses it in the Temple courts and takes hold of a whip to chase
out the moneychangers – wow, this is nearer to home!

In this story, we are confronted with the power of a Jesus who
feels as we often feel; a Jesus who is tired as we are often tired;
a Jesus who would rather just go home and put his feet up for
a well-earned rest. But there it is, right in front of him – a person
who needs what he has to offer, and there's no way Jesus will
ignore him. So he calls blind Bartimaeus to him, and says,
'Look, what do you want from me?' I love this Jesus. And I give
thanks to God for coming to this world in him – for coming
among us in a way that we can grasp, in a person we can understand.

And then of course, after we see this story possibly from
Jesus' perspective, there's 'Bartimaeus the Blind', or as his
friends might have called him, 'Big-Mouth Bartimaeus'. This
man is intense, as he sits there by the roadside. As soon as he
hears Jesus is coming, he starts yelling. He wants to make sure
Jesus can hear him, however close or far away he might be.
'Jesus, son of David, have mercy on me.'

Now we need to understand that this title, 'son of David' is
the key here. It's not like him yelling, 'Jesus, son of Joseph, have
mercy on me!' No. It's a bit more intense than that. When
Bartimaeus addresses Jesus as the son of David, he's referring
to a Messianic title. He's pointing out Jesus' royal lineage, which
is a marker of his standing as the Messiah. He's saying, 'I know
who you are really. I know that you are the one that was sent by
God, the Messiah. I know you can do anything.'

It's easy for us to read this story and miss the fact that Blind
Bartimaeus knows who he is dealing with here. He knows he
won't give up, so he keeps trying in the only way he can. He calls
out to the son of David, the Holy one of God, and keeps on

until he finally gets an answer. I know that Jesus tells him that his faith has made him well, and I believe that. But there is another ingredient to the healing of Bartimaeus – I believe his persistence also made him well. After all, what would have happened if he had just said, 'Er, excuse me Jesus, have you got a minute?' Surely that's what everyone would have been saying. It would have been physically impossible – there just wouldn't have been time for a man to stop for a minute to every single person calling out for attention. After all, there would be thousands of people in Jericho, let alone all the others who were following Jesus.

Bartimaeus is persistent. He's relentless, and in a way, he's insisting on his own healing. He's not going to let the Messiah get away. Even though people were trying shut him up, he won't be quiet. 'Jesus, son of David! Have mercy on me!' 'Jesus, son of David! Have mercy on me!' I wonder how long you or I would keep it up?

What does this say about the way we relate to God? I think this story is powerful because of the two things I have mentioned. I think this story dares us to jump in and put our arms around a very, very human Jesus. This story dares us to encounter God's presence in the most vulnerable and human intersection that we can imagine. And isn't this the point when it comes down to God in Christ Jesus? We have a fully human Jesus and a persistent follower. A human Jesus, and someone seeking the touch of God who won't give up. Are we persistent in our search for God's touch in our own lives? Are we prepared to keep calling on the name of God in Jesus Christ, even when we don't think were getting an answer? Do we keep moving, keep trying? Are we able to stop, take a deep breath, utter a prayer, and renew our commitment to God? Can we look afresh at this very human and wonderful Jesus, and come with new eyes, new hope, and a new life to the side of the road and sit with Bartimaeus while we yell together, 'Jesus, Son of David! Have mercy on us?' And when he turns and asks us what we want him to do, will we say, 'Just let us see again.' 'Just give us vision.' 'Just ground in us your healing and renewing love.'?

And when our faith has made us well, let's get up and follow.

7

Jesus Heals a Centurion's Servant
A story about faith

Luke 7:1–10

After Jesus had finished all his sayings in the hearing of the people, he entered Capernaum. A centurion there had a slave whom he valued highly, and who was ill and close to death. When he heard about Jesus, he sent some Jewish elders to him, asking him to come and heal his slave. When they came to Jesus, they appealed to him earnestly, saying, 'He is worthy of having you do this for him, for he loves our people, and it is he who built our synagogue for us.' And Jesus went with them, but when he was not far from the house, the centurion sent friends to say to him, 'Lord, do not trouble yourself, for I am not worthy to have you come under my roof; therefore I did not presume to come to you. But only speak the word and let my servant be healed. For I also am a man set under authority, with soldiers under me; and I say to one, "Go," and he goes, and to another, "Come," and he comes, and to my slave, "Do this," and the slave does it.' When Jesus heard this, he was amazed at him, and turning to the crowd that followed him, he said, 'I tell you, not even in Israel have I found such faith.' When those who had been sent returned to the house, they found the slave in good health.

In this Gospel story, the main character (apart from Jesus) is an unlikely role model for faith. After all, he was an officer in the army of a foreign power that had conquered the nation. He was an army officer, whose main responsibility would be to enforce the laws and policies of a foreign power. So we are talking about an enemy of the Jews, a man who would normally be despised. And yet, this man had such a profound faith in God that he even amazed Jesus.

And what an example for us! When we look at our own lives – well, some of us are only too well aware of the mess we make of things; some of us are haunted by guilt and regret for the things we have done wrong, or the good we've failed to do. But what a comfort it is to remember from this story that no one is outside the limits of God's grace. Not even an enemy army officer! The grace made available to that officer of a brutal army that had conquered and occupied the land is also available to you and me. How we can thank God, that living by faith isn't merely a matter of keeping the rules. But let's go to the punch-line of the story. Jesus, speaking about this Roman army officer said he hadn't seen such faith in all of Israel. This man, who many would assume was the enemy, is in fact a role model for living by faith.

So what can we learn from the story? Well, it's clearly shown that the Roman officer was compassionate. This can be seen in his obvious concern for his slave whom he highly valued and who was terminally ill. This officer did what he could to find healing for the slave. Now I realise that some might say when he sent for Jesus to heal the slave, this was not so much compassion, but rather a matter of economics. After all, it says the officer 'highly valued' his slave. This could imply that the slave was worth a lot of money and the officer is merely concerned to protect his investment. Surely this can't be the right interpretation, after all, to 'highly value' a person doesn't always mean monetary value. When we say we highly value our husband, or wife, or a friend we are not talking about financial worth. But what about this business of owning a slave? This story reminds us that living by faith is possible even in an imperfect world, and even though we are not perfect.

At the time of Jesus, slavery was normal in that society. None of the New Testament writers questioned the rights or wrongs about owning slaves. We, however, realise now that slavery is a violation of God's will. All men, women and children were created to be free; no one has been created as property to be owned by another person. All are created free children of God.

In this story, when the officer heard about Jesus' ministry, and he learned that he was in the area, he asked some of the religious leaders in the community (the elders from the local synagogue), to go and ask Jesus to please come and heal his slave. Clearly there is both faith and love expressed in this request. When the religious leaders approach Jesus, they don't simply deliver the officer's request. Luke tells us they appealed to Jesus 'earnestly'. They didn't merely do what they were asked to do; they personally interceded on behalf of the Roman officer. Listen to what they said, 'He is worthy of having you do this for him, for he loves our people, and it was he who built our synagogue for us.' 'He loves our people' – a significant symbol of that love is that he built the synagogue for the community where he was stationed. He, a Roman, built a place to worship God, a place to study the Scriptures, a place to learn about God and God's will, a place that would serve his neighbours. Why would he do such a thing? 'He loves us,' said the elders.

I think this army officer was, what the Jews of that day would call, 'a God-fearer', that is, a Gentile who believed what the Jews believed, but who had not been circumcised, and who didn't follow the strict dietary laws. He believed in the God of the Jews, and was committed to him, even though he wasn't a Jew himself. And I believe that it was his faith and hope that motivated him to request the leaders of the synagogue to ask Jesus to come and heal his slave.

We are not told what Jesus said in response to the request – it simply says he went with them. Anyhow, Jesus was almost at the address when some other friends of the officer came to meet Jesus with another message. They tell him not to trouble himself by coming to the officer's house. The officer had told them to say that he was not worthy of having Jesus enter his home. This is an interesting contrast. The religious leaders, who had pleaded with Jesus to come, had said he was worthy because of his love and generosity, and yet the officer says he's not worthy. What an example of humility! After all, we are talking about a centurion soldier who was in command of a hundred men who were trained fighters – brutal warriors. It would take a strong, confident, tough and disciplined officer to command and maintain order among such men. He would have to be a no-nonsense person who could and would send men into battle, and send many of them to their death. Obviously the officer would have realised that Jesus, as a Jew, would have defiled himself by going into the house of a Gentile, but I think it was more than this. I think it really was an act of humility.

True humility is only possible where strength and power exists, otherwise there's nothing to be humble about. I don't think he was simply being diplomatic, or he was suffering from low self-esteem. What was at the heart of his humility was his commitment to God, and his confidence and faith in the grace of God.

He was confident enough to believe that all Jesus needed to do was to 'say the word' (give the order), and the slave would be healed. No wonder Jesus was amazed! And we are told that when the messengers returned home, they discovered the slave had been healed – without Jesus even going there! What a wonderful lesson for us.

Sadly, there are many who long for God to work a miracle of something new in their lives who yet feel a nagging sense of unworthiness. How it must grieve the Lord's heart of love to see us hold back from him, because we can't believe that he could love us enough to give us something new. But Jesus came to show that 'God so loved the world . . .' – saint and sinner, you and me!

I meet so many whose faith in the power of God gets diminished because they still carry guilt from things of the past, and who can't bring themselves to accept that God has forgiven them – that the slate has been wiped clean. There are others who feel utterly unworthy and not fit to receive the blessings God has in store for them, because they don't feel good enough. They aren't as spiritual as they think they ought to be. They don't pray enough; they don't read their Bible enough; they are not as regular in their church attendance as they ought to be.

The Gospel stories reassure us that God doesn't wait until everything is us is perfect before he will act. Thankfully, he accepts us as we are, not as we think we should be. Jesus is motivated by love and compassion, not by rules and regulations.

So, as we approach the living God and we ask his blessing on us, and for others too, we come with words of faith on our lips – 'Lord, I am not worthy to receive you but say the word only and my soul shall be healed.'

8

Jesus Heals a Crippled Woman
People always come first

Luke 13:10–17

Now Jesus was teaching in one of the synagogues on the sabbath. And just then there appeared a woman with a spirit that had crippled her for eighteen years. She was bent over and was quite unable to stand up straight. When Jesus saw her, he called her over and said, 'Woman, you are set free from your ailment.' When he laid his hands on her, immediately she stood up straight and began praising God. But the leader of the synagogue, indignant because Jesus had cured on the sabbath, kept saying to the crowd, 'There are six days on which work ought to be done; come on those days and be cured, and not on the sabbath day.' But the Lord answered him and said, 'You hypocrites! Does not each of you on the sabbath untie his ox or his donkey from the manger, and lead it away to give it water? And ought not this woman, a daughter of Abraham whom Satan bound for eighteen long years, be set free from this bondage on the sabbath day?' When he said this, all his opponents were put to shame; and the entire crowd was rejoicing at all the wonderful things that he was doing.

I read once of an experiment where a fish was placed in an aquarium and it was free to swim from one end to the other. After a while, a glass divider was placed in the aquarium, so that the fish could only swim in one half of the aquarium. To begin with the fish, still thinking it had the free run of the aquarium, kept bumping into the glass divider. After a while the fish learnt that it was confined to swimming in just one half of the aquarium. Eventually the glass divider was removed, allowing the fish once again full access to the whole aquarium. But the fish continued thereafter to swim in only half of the aquarium. It had grown used to the conditions that had been placed on it and, even though the conditions no longer existed, it continued to live as if they did.

That speaks to me of the situation that so many people find themselves in today. There seems to be a strong human need to control and dominate our own lives. Generally speaking, we find it difficult to accept any elements of reality that come from beyond us. I guess we want to be in control so that we can pretend we are in charge.

I think we are like the fish in the aquarium. So often we have restricted our world unnecessarily. We have set our own divider in place, making our own world small enough so that we can have the illusion that we are in control.

The message of the gospels is that there is a power and purpose which can break in on our limited everyday existence in this world; that things can be changed and transformed, whether we acknowledge it or not. We can choose to ignore it, or even to resist it, and thereby remain in only half of the aquarium, or we can welcome it and discover the freedom of a larger and more fulfilling way of living.

In the Gospel reading, we heard of the woman with a bad

back. We can picture her, making her way down the cobbled stone street. She's bent over at the waist. Not just bent over, the Bible says she was 'bent double.' She was bent over where her torso almost pressed against her knees. She would waddle down the street, and people would stare. Children would mock her, and she would hear the whispers.

This was no ordinary back problem; she had suffered with this deformity for eighteen long years. I wonder what caused it – an injury, or a fall of some kind? Whatever it was, her twisted muscles and misplaced vertebrae had brought her to this horrible state.

This woman was a good woman, and we know this, because Jesus calls her a 'daughter of Abraham.' This wasn't simply a reference to her being Jewish; it was a reference to her righteousness. We can tell she was a good woman by where we find her. She was in the synagogue – she was in the house of God. She was there to worship the Lord on the Lord's Day, the Sabbath. And it would have been no easy thing for her. To get there, she had to make her way down the streets. She had to face the stares, the whispers and the taunts of children. It would have been a slow and painful journey from her home to the house of God, but she didn't let anything stop her.

As she walked those streets, unable to look beyond a few feet ahead, waddling from side to side, people would stop and stare. She could hear them – 'She must have done a terrible thing . . . It's God's curse . . . What a pity.' But she was going to the house of God; she was going to seek the presence of the living God! Little did she know that day, as she hobbled into the synagogue, that this was not just another Sabbath. This was to be her day. This was the day that God was going to give her a new life.

Jesus is in the synagogue; he is sitting down and teaching. A scroll is brought to him, but Jesus looks up and his eyes scan the congregation. His eyes are drawn to the woman with the bad back. And that doesn't surprise us, does it? That's the way it is with Jesus. His eyes are always focusing on hurting people, people with a need. Yes, he sees this woman and suddenly the scroll isn't as important anymore. He sees one of God's children hurting and in pain. He recognises the hardship, the pain, the suffering of this little woman and his heart is filled with compassion. Jesus stands up, and the crowd is uneasy. What's he doing? – they wonder. Jesus calls the woman to come forward. 'Woman, daughter of Abraham, come over here, to me.' The woman realises he is speaking to her, and she begins to make her way to him. Every eye in that synagogue is fixed on the woman as she struggles forward. She stands there in front of Jesus, bowed low, like a servant before a king.

Jesus reaches out and touches her back and tells her she's free from this curse. And the writer tells us, immediately she straightened up. She springs up with the cry, 'Praise the Lord!' She's leaping in the air, twirling around, shouting praises to God, glorifying God. What a miracle! The crowd are on their feet too, and here comes the ruler of the synagogue – he must be rejoicing too. No he isn't! He's hopping mad. You could hear the anger as he turns to the woman and then the crowd, 'What are you doing? There are six days to be healed. This is the Sabbath!'

He doesn't see a woman set free from eighteen years of bondage, he sees a rule that has been broken. He sees things that disagree with his theology and his conceptions about God. He misses the miracle and sees a supposed broken law. And you can almost hear him, 'My God doesn't act like this! This isn't of God, this is wrong!'

It makes me think – we had better be careful what we say isn't of God. Jesus was there to teach them about God, but his teaching didn't come from the scroll but from his actions. He could have healed that woman on any day, but he didn't. He healed on this day, the Sabbath, to teach them a very important lesson. Just listen to what he said. 'You hypocrites! You call yourself righteous, religious leaders. You care more about your animals than you do this daughter of Abraham. You'll free an animal; you'll feed and water and care for your animals on the Sabbath, yet you would prefer to leave this woman in pain.' But what is he saying?

Jesus is saying that people are more important than rules. People, hurting people, always come first with God. God is concerned far more about ministry to people than about traditions, customs and poorly understood laws. There are people who will read this book, bent over by the load of so many things. For most of us, on the outside, everything looks fine, but on the inside – many of us are bent over in pain, or frustration or anxiety or sorrow, and deep down we know we need a touch from God.

Here is a word of truth – God is present now, just as he was in the synagogue on that Sabbath day. And whatever circumstances of life may be weighing you down, God sees your pain and he cares, and wants to touch you.

When Jesus called the woman to come to him, she didn't hesitate, she came. She had no idea what was going to happen, but she was there to meet God, and when he called, she answered. Like this woman, we could let all kinds of things stop us from coming: we could let our own ideas about what God should do and how he should do it, hold us back; we could let our own theological misconceptions hold us back; we could let our doubts hold us back . . . Or, like the woman, we can let God be God and trust him. He would never hurt us, for he only wants the best for us.

You know, we live in an aquarium that is much larger than we would allow it to be. The Christian faith testifies that Jesus is still alive and present with us now. By his own spiritual presence within each of us, we have access to a new freedom, a new power, and a new life. And yet so many of us set up an imaginary glass divider that restricts and holds us back. The Holy

Spirit of God has removed the dividers. Things don't have to stay the way they have always been. We are the ones who have put the restrictions on our lives. It's an illusion that there is no reality beyond the one we already know.

Week by week, as we meet together with fellow believers, we don't do so out of a sense of obligation. We meet in joyous expectation that the Holy one of God will be with us, invading our little world in order to enlarge it. And there are countless numbers who will testify that they were not disappointed, for they have found that his promises are true.

And it can be so for each of us today.

9

A Girl Restored to Life and a Woman Healed

Jesus saw the invisible

Luke 8:40–56

Now when Jesus returned, the crowd welcomed him, for they were all waiting for him. Just then there came a man named Jairus, a leader of the synagogue. He fell at Jesus' feet and begged him to come to his house, for he had an only daughter, about twelve years old, who was dying.

As he went, the crowds pressed in on him. Now there was a woman who had been suffering from haemorrhages for twelve years; and though she had spent all she had on physicians, no one could cure her. She came up behind him and touched the fringe of his clothes, and immediately here haemorrhage stopped. The Jesus asked, 'Who touched me?' When all denied it, Peter said, 'Master, the crowds surround you and press in on you.' But Jesus said, 'Someone touched me; for I noticed that power had gone out from me.' When the woman saw that she could not remain hidden, she came trembling; and falling down before him, she declared in the presence of all the people why she had touched him, and how she had been immediately healed. He said to her, 'Daughter, your faith has made you well; go in peace.'

While he was still speaking, someone came from the leader's house to say, 'Your daughter is dead; do not trouble the teacher any longer.' When Jesus heard this, he replied, 'Do not fear. Only believe, and she will be saved.' When he came to the house, he did not allow anyone to enter with him, except Peter, John, and James, and the child's father and mother. They were all weeping and wailing for her; but he said, 'Do not weep; for she is not dead but sleeping.' And they laughed at him, knowing that she was dead. But he took her by the hand and called out, 'Child, get up!' Her spirit returned, and she got up at once. Then he directed them to give her something to eat. Her parents were astounded; but he ordered them to tell no one what had happened.

Right, so here we have Jesus, at the height of his popularity healing Jairus' daughter. Jairus, we know was a rather important person – a ruler of the synagogue, and Jesus is having to push through the crowds to reach his house. And then there was that touch – a purposeful touch, that drains away power from Jesus. Just a little power, but enough for Jesus to notice, and he turns round. 'Who touched me?' And there she is, this elderly woman. She doesn't say what was wrong, but from the furtive way she's behaving, you can tell it's something unclean. And the people in the crowd are pretty indignant that someone who is unclean should have dared to touch anyone, let alone Jesus. Anyhow, power went out from him, so whatever had been wrong, in whoever touched him, must have been healed. Just imagine what faith she must have had to reach out and touch the hem of his garment! No wonder Jesus says, 'Go in peace; your faith has made you well.'

They carry on down the road. Then messengers come from

Jairus' house, 'It's too late; she's dead! No need to bother now.' But Jesus says, 'Don't be afraid, have faith, she'll get well!' So he goes into the house – just Jesus, Jairus and his wife, Peter, James and John. And he takes her by the hand and she gets up. And then Jesus says, 'Well, don't just stand there, give her something to eat!'

There's so much we can learn from this wonderful episode, but for me, one of the most important things is that 'Jesus sees the invisible.'

Did you notice that neither of the two main characters in this story have names? The two who were healed are known simply as 'Jairus' daughter' and 'the woman with a haemorrhage'. But of course this shouldn't surprise us, because they were women. As happens so often in the Bible, women had no status in the Jewish communities. They were seen as unimportant, and so the biblical writers more often than not, didn't even bother to record their names. It's the men who get their names mentioned, not women. When we read the story of the feeding of the five thousand, we are told that there were five thousand men there, that's not counting the women and the children! You see, they literally didn't count. They were invisible!

So the two women in this story are invisible people. Jairus' daughter was only a child. You will know people grew up quickly in those days – a boy was considered a man when he was thirteen, but this girl was only twelve. Here in England, she would be half-way through her secondary education. But at the time of Jesus, she wouldn't have been allowed any academic teaching; that was strictly for her brothers. Women weren't considered capable of any academic learning. That's why it's so shocking that Mary of Bethany sat at Jesus' feet listening to him. Martha wasn't only distressed that she had been left to get on with the domestic chores by herself, but she knew it wasn't proper for Mary to be listening to Jesus like that!

Jairus' daughter was only a child, and that made her invisible!

The woman with the haemorrhage – well she was unclean and that made her invisible too! Women were considered unclean when they bled, and she poor soul, had been bleeding for twelve years. (Now that's interesting – it was the same length of time that Jairus' daughter had been living. I wonder if there's anything significant in that number?). The point was that this woman had to live outside the community, and couldn't join in anything. It was just the same as if she had leprosy. She was, to all intents and purposes, invisible, just like the little girl.

Jesus came, and saw the invisible ones. He saw them and he healed them. I wonder who the invisible people are in our society today? I suppose there are lots who come under that heading. Bus drivers for example – we get on the bus, we flash our pass or pay our money, and barely notice that it's a human being driving that bus. Or we go to the supermarket – we wait, sometimes impatiently, as the person behind the checkout moves our shopping over the laser beam, and then we hand over our loyalty card and cash or credit card, and we can do it without seeing there's a person there. There are so many invisible people around us, aren't there? They sit in the pew in front of us at church; some are even related to us.

Jesus always saw the invisible. He saw them, and met them where they needed him. But he didn't only see the invisibles; he also touched the untouchables. I've already mentioned the woman with a haemorrhage being unclean. She absolutely ought never to have touched Jesus, because just by touching him, she polluted him and made him unclean too. She could have expected Jesus to be angry with her because, strictly speaking, he would have to go and spend a day in isolation and have a bath before he could go back into the community. And you know, the main reason they told Jesus not to bother going to Jairus' house now that the little girl had died, was that Jesus couldn't go in there without making himself unclean.

But Jesus never seems to give a hoot about whether he's

unclean or not. He allows the woman to touch him, he takes the little girl by the hand; and from other stories, we know he touched lepers, visited Gentiles in their home, and generally ignored the ceremonial rules and regulations in a way that outrages the religious establishment of the day.

Who are the untouchables today? Who are those that we would prefer not to be seen with them, in case we are judged to be like them? The ones who take drugs, or who drink too much, or who like different sexual partners, those who many would call the fringe people? Or could they just be people who are a bit different from the majority, those who are always critical perhaps, or who are always moaning, or the loners, or the handicapped?

Jesus sees the invisible, and touches the untouchables, because he treats everyone as an individual of infinite value. He doesn't classify people, lumping them into invisible and untouchable groups – he sees the uniqueness in each of us.

Sometimes I feel invisible and sometimes untouchable. And I guess you do too. No one can know the isolation you feel sometimes; no one has the same fears you have about yourself, or about someone you love, or perhaps about the future. No one knows the weakness or inadequacy you feel; no one knows what it's like to be you or me. But Jesus does! For no one is invisible or untouchable to him. That's why we are here today. For he sees each one of us – yes, he sees everything about us and, as he looks, he sees each one of us as his precious child, and offers to touch us with his healing and compassionate hand.

10

Jesus Cleanses a Leper
A meditation

Mark 1:40–45

A leper came to Jesus begging him, and kneeling he said to him, 'If you choose, you can make me clean.' Moved with pity, Jesus stretched out his hand and touched him, and said to him, 'I do choose. Be made clean!' Immediately the leprosy left him, and he was made clean. After sternly warning him he sent him away at once, saying to him, 'See that you say nothing to anyone; but go, show yourself to the priest, and offer for your cleansing what Moses commanded, as a testimony to them.' But he went out and began to proclaim it freely and to spread the word, so that Jesus could no longer go into a town openly, but stayed out in the country; and people came to him from every quarter.

It hadn't entered his head that he would become a leper. He found the first spot one morning when he was washing. It was so small, he felt it couldn't be anything at all. Certainly nothing to worry about! But, over the next few months, before his eyes, it grew and grew.

There wasn't any good reason why he should tell anyone. It wouldn't make any difference. He would simply be making a fuss over nothing. But one morning, as he kissed his wife and cuddled his little daughter, he suddenly realised their danger, the danger, that through touching him, they too might become lepers. Could he condemn them to that? He who loved them so much! Quietly, he began to put his affairs in order, sorting out his possessions, sorting out his finances. He had to make sure that for them, everything would be all right.

Finally, the day came. He had been dreading the day he had to tell his wife, 'My dear, I have to go away.' As he looked at her, the person he loved best in all the world, he didn't know how he would live without her. 'Darling, it's so very hard for me to tell you this, but I have to go. You see, I'm a leper!' As he left, he broke his heart.

In the years that followed, his heart was broken many more times, for the life of a leper was hard. There was little food, little comfort, and what was worst of all, little hope. For leprosy was incurable.

Sometimes he thought he would go mad. Why had he been born, simply to wait day by day for death to release him? Was this all he could expect? Would he never again see a friendly face? Would he never again feel that somebody cared?

Many years ago, a woman who lived in the dock-lands of the East End of London went, on an impulse, to a woman's meeting at the local church. She had been living with a Chinese sailor and had a small baby by him. She took the baby to the meeting with her. She found that she enjoyed the meeting so much and so started to attend it regularly. But one day, the pastor arrived on her doorstep. He said, 'I'm afraid I must ask you to stop coming to the women's meeting at the church.' She was stunned, 'But why?' The pastor explained, 'Well, it's the other women. They don't approve of your lifestyle, and have said they'll stop coming if you insist on being there.' The woman felt so sad. She said, 'But pastor, I know I'm a sinner, but isn't there anywhere a sinner can go?'

There wasn't anywhere a leper could go. As the disease took hold of him, so his skin thickened, and his face changed so that he didn't look like a man at all. He became so disfigured – even his own mother wouldn't recognise him now. He spent his days wandering aimlessly. He took to visiting the villages late at night and in the early hours of the morning, just on the off-chance that he might hear another human voice. It was on one of these visits that he overheard a conversation. They were talking about a man called Jesus – Jesus of Nazareth, a teacher and a healer.

As he listened, for the first time in many years, the leper felt a small flame of hope light up in his heart. Could it be true? Had Jesus really healed all those people? And if this Jesus had healed others, couldn't he heal him? But it was against the law for a leper to approach any ordinary person, and he could be stoned if he tried it. Was it worth it? How much did he want to be healed?

Two friends were going swimming, and amongst the subjects they were discussing, they began to discuss religion. Just as they were walking into the sea for a swim, one said to the other, 'What wouldn't I give to find a real faith in God?' 'Ah, but how much do you want it?' his friend replied. 'Oh, very much, very much indeed,' he said. And then to his amazement, his friend suddenly grabbed him and pushed his head under the water. In spite of the man's struggles, he held his head under water until he nearly drowned. When he released his grip, the man stood up, coughing and spluttering and gasping for breath. 'What on earth did you do that for?' The man asked. His friend said, 'What was it that you wanted most in the world just now?' 'Why air of course, I couldn't breathe!' 'Well,' said his friend, 'When you want a real faith in God as much as you wanted air just now, that's when you'll find it!'

The leper wanted to be healed, more than he's ever wanted anything. Yes, and for that, he'd risk being stoned; he'd risk being rejected; but would Jesus want to heal him? It took some days before he could find Jesus, and then at last he saw him. He could have cried with relief. He ran forward and fell at Jesus' feet. 'Sir,' he said, 'If you want to, you can make me clean.'

Jesus looked down at this kneeling figure, a leper, covered in dirty old rags; shapeless, smelly and repulsive – hardly a man at all really. Gently Jesus took away the cloth that hid the leper's face, he touched all the deformities that the leprosy had made, and looked deep into the man's eyes. 'Of course I want to,' he said, 'Be clean!' Then he took the leper's hands in his own and raised him to his feet.

When Jesus enters a situation, things change. He touches the untouchable. Jesus looked beyond the deformities and simply saw a man in desperate need. Where there is real need, Jesus will always involve himself.

The leper was certain that Jesus could help him, if only he wanted to. And Jesus left him in no doubt that he did want to, just as we should be in no doubt that he wants to meet us in our need too. The help we receive from him, may not always be what we had hoped for, but the love and the power that healed a leper is still at work today. When we invite his intervention, something always happens.

When bad things happen to us we are tempted to forget – to forget how much Jesus loves us, and how much he wants what is best for us, and that his love and power can transform the most hopeless situations.

'Sir', said the leper, 'if you want to, you can make me clean.' 'I do want to.' said Jesus, 'Be clean!'

May each of us be brought into a deeper and more meaningful relationship of love with him, that we also might be transformed.